GEOLOGIC GUIDE TO

CUMBERLAND ISLAND

NATIONAL SEASHORE

Prepared for the
United States Department of Interior
as part of Contract No. CX5000-8-1563

DEPARTMENT OF NATURAL RESOURCES
Joe D. Tanner, Commissioner

ENVIRONMENTAL PROTECTION DIVISION
J. Leonard Ledbetter, Division Director

GEORGIA GEOLOGIC SURVEY
William H. McLemore, State Geologist

Atlanta
Reprinted 1991

Era	Period	Epoch	Stages	Began years ago	Dominant life and important events
Cenozoic	Quaternary	Recent (Holocene)		11,000	man
		Pleistocene	Wisconsin	0.2 million	glacial
			Sangamonian	0.4 "	interglacial
			Illinoisian	0.6 "	glacial
			Yarmouthian	0.9 "	interglacial
			Kansan	1.4 "	glacial
			Aftonian	1.7 "	interglacial
			Nebraskan	3.0 "	glacial
	Tertiary	Pliocene		6 million	
		Miocene		22 "	
		Oligocene		37 "	mammals
		Eocene		54 "	
		Paleocene		62 "	
Mesozoic	Cretaceous			130 million	
	Jurassic			180 "	reptiles
	Triassic			230 "	
Paleozoic	Permian			280 million	
	Pennsylvanian			325 "	amphibians
	Mississippian			340 "	trees
	Devonian			400 "	grasses
	Silurian			450 "	fish
	Ordovician			500 "	
	Cambrian			580 "	invertebrates
Precambrian				1.8 billion	development of oxygen in atmosphere; appearance of eucaryotic cells
				2+ billion	life originated as a procaryote cell
				3+ billion	formation of ocean
				4+ billion	oldest rocks
				5+ billion	origin of earth and solar system
				12 billion	origin of the universe according to the present rate of expansion

GEOLOGIC TIME CHART

2

CONTENTS

Introduction   5

Geologic Trail Guide   12

Conclusion   34

Acknowledgements   34

Bibliography   35

Glossary   36

(Italicized words in the text are listed in the glossary.)

INTRODUCTION

umberland Island, internationally renowned for its spectacular beauty, is also distinguished s the largest, the southernmost, and one of the least disturbed *barrier islands* fringing the tlantic coast of Georgia. Barrier islands, so called because they form a protective barrier etween the mainland and the open seas, are a common feature worldwide. Geologically, :umberland Island is an interesting feature because it is formed of both an ancient 'leistocene barrier island and a modern Holocene beach dune zone (see Geologic Time :hart). The seaward Holocene portion of the island has been welded by wave action onto he ancient Pleistocene part of the island.

)uring the "Ice Ages" of the Pleistocene Epoch, sea level fluctuated significantly as the ontinental glaciers advanced and retreated. Each time that there was *a still-stand,* or a elatively constant sea level, a shoreline consisting of barrier islands and related marshes ormed. This has resulted in a series of terraces in the lower Georgia Coastal Plain, each of vhich originated as a barrier island chain. The "core" of Cumberland Island formed about 0,000 years ago at the late Pleistocene still-stand known as Silver Bluff, when sea level was bout 1.4 m (4 1/2 ft) higher than present.

about 25,000 years ago, the growth of the Pleistocene continental glaciers resulted in a vorldwide lowering of sea level. Pleistocene Cumberland Island, the adjacent salt marshes, nd 129 km (80 mi) of continental shelf were literally left high and dry as the seas slowly vithdrew for several thousand years. Island and salt marsh deposits were exposed to veathering and erosion for the next 15,000 to 20,000 years, as sea level stabilized some 122 n (400 ft) below the modern sea level.

some 11,000 years ago, the Holocene Epoch was initiated by the worldwide retreat of :ontinental ice sheets. Rising seas rapidly engulfed the Pleistocene Coastal Plain until sea evel again stabilized slightly lower than present about 5,000 years ago. The Holocene)ortion of Cumberland then formed a short distance seaward of the present shoreline. As ea level again began a slow rise, the barrier island sediments were reworked and forced andward (fig. 1), initiating the landward movement of barrier islands still in progress in most :oastal regions of the world. In time, wave action welded the sands of the Holocene island :hain onto the preexisting Pleistocene barrier island system of the Georgia coastline.

rhus, Cumberland Island is composed of a large, central "core" of Pleistocene barrier island sediments and a narrow, seaward veneer of Holocene sands. Because the relative rate of sea evel rise has been about 15-30 cm. (6-12 in.) per century for the last 3,000 years, Cumberland Island is still slowly moving landward.

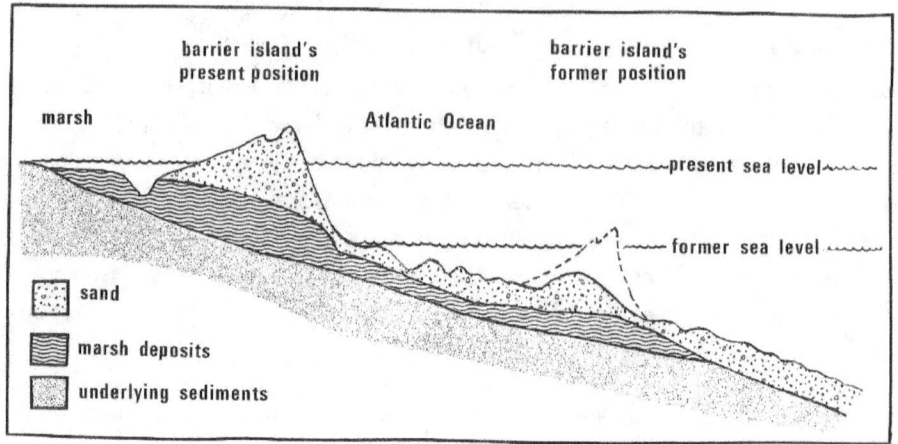

Figure 1. Origin of the Holocene barrier island system. This figure indicates that the Holocene portion of Cumberland Island originally formed during the "Ice Ages" at a lower stand of sea level. When glacial meltwater caused the oceans to rise, wave action forced the Holocene island to its present location, that is, welded onto the older Pleistocene "core" of Cumberland Island.

Throughout its geologic history, the island has undergone constant modification due to effects of erosion, deposition, and biologic growth. In the vast reaches of geologic time, this island is an extremely young and unstable geologic feature. Like all barrier islands, Cumberland is constantly in the state of change that only appears "unnatural" to man when his structures are threatened.

One of the most important aspects of a coastal region is whether the sea is rising, sinking, or stable with respect to land. The Georgia coast is classified as a "depositional coast" because the land surface is down-warping, or slowly sinking (i.e. the sea is rising). The broad, low Coastal Plain of Georgia is marked by large, long rivers emptying into the sea. The depositional setting of a coastal zone is strongly related to plate tectonics, the movements of the plates which form the crust of the earth. Most coastlines may be described as either a collision or a trailing edge coast (fig. 2). A collision coast, where two plates converge, is characterized by rapid uplift, young mountain ranges and short rivers; for example, the California coast is classified as "collision." A trailing edge coast, such as the eastern U.S. coast, is relatively stable and forms a "depositional" coast. It is on such coastlines that barrier islands are most frequently found.

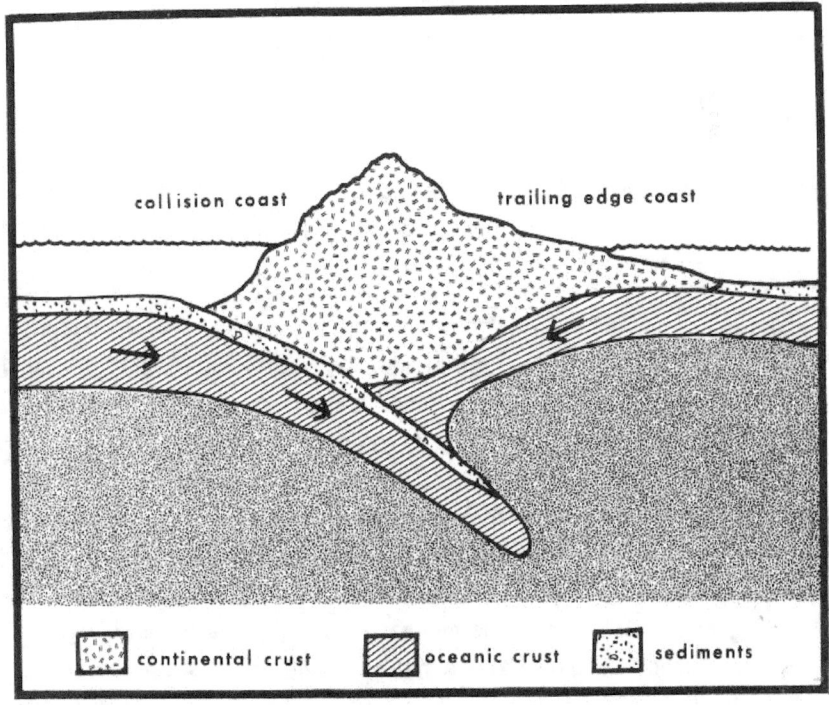

Figure 2. Diagram representing collision and trailing edge coasts.
Arrows indicate the direction of movement of crustal plates.

oday, Cumberland Island is sculpted by wave action and tidal currents, the extent of which
 directly related to tidal range, the difference between successive high and low tides.
arrier islands are rare on tide-dominated coasts, where tidal range exceeds 4 m (13 ft).
long coastlines of smaller tidal range, such as the Gulf coast, barrier islands are long,
near features with few tidal inlets; these islands are said to be "wave dominated."

slands shaped by a moderate tidal range of 2-4 m (6-13 ft), as is Cumberland Island, are
tunted and shorter. They are characterized by wide tidal inlets to accommodate the large
idal exchange throughout the tidal cycle and by well developed ebb tidal deltas. These
nderwater accumulations of sand, built by the falling tide, serve as vital sand storage
reas; unfortunately, they create serious navigational hazards as well. Coasts of moderate
idal range are said to be in a "mixed energy" environment since they are shaped by both
vave and tidal currents. Cumberland Island, with a tidal range of 2-3 m (6-9 ft), possesses
he "drum stick" shape (fig. 3) that typically develops in such a mixed energy

environment.

Cumberland Island (fig. 4) is about 26 km (16 mi) long and about 4.5 km (3 mi) wide at its greatest width. (Little Cumberland Island, the northern portion of the island, is privately owned and not a part of Cumberland Island National Seashore.) At its highest point, it is approximately 17 m (50 ft) above sea level. The island is composed of a series of modified beach ridges and backed by extensive salt marshes. Generally speaking, its four major divisions are: (1) an actively changing Holocene beach dune zone, (2) the interior of the island, composed of vegetated Pleistocene beach ridges, (3) the tidal inlets that bound the island north and south, and (4) the salt marsh/tidal channel area that surrounds the back barrier, or landward portion of the island.

The erosional and depositional history of Cumberland Island is closely tied to the processes associated with its neighboring tidal inlets, St. Andrew Sound and the St. Marys Entrance. St Andrew Sound, the northern boundary of the island, is the largest inlet in Georgia, for here the Satilla, the Little Satilla, and the Cumberland Rivers meet the Atlantic. This inlet has been considerably modified over time by inlet migration. Inlet migration results when a river or tidal inlet channel shifts its position in response to underwater sand deposition. These shifts generally cause the northern (updrift) end of barrier islands to be unstable. Due to jetty construction at the southern St. Marys Entrance, the island has enlarged here approximately 2 km^2 (494 acres) since the late 1800's. The mid-barrier straight beach has changed far less since 1843; this is the barrier island beach zone that is typically the most stable (see fig. 19).

The interior of the island is composed of the Pleistocene vegetated beach ridges that formed when sea level was falling and Cumberland Island was building seaward. Where these ridges are largely undisturbed, as those directly behind the present day dune fields in central and northern Cumberland Island, they are typically vegetated by a mature maritime forest dominated by live oaks and palmettos. The original dune shape is preserved. Many small freshwater ponds are found in the depressions between these ancient dunes. Farther inland the ridges have been so modified by logging, agriculture, and overgrazing that their original character cannot easily be discerned.

The entire western boundary of the island is surrounded by extensive salt marshes and tidal creeks with the Cumberland River forming the major western boundary. In the *low marsh* which lies between the high and low tide marks, the hardy long cordgrass (*Spartina alterniflora*) flourishes in this harsh environment. In the *high marsh*, a zone generally above high tide but occasionally wetted by storm and spring tides, the black needlerush (*Juncus roemerianus*), predominates. Oysters are abundant on the numerous tidal flats in the marsh zone.

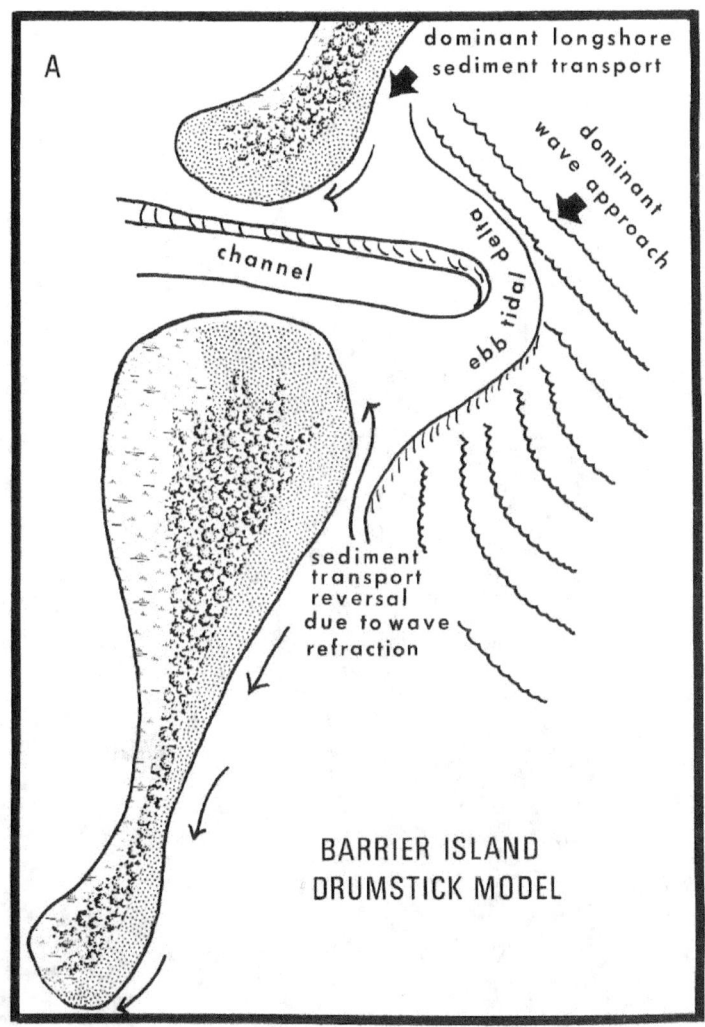

Figure 3. Barrier island "drumstick model" typical along coasts of moderate tidal range.

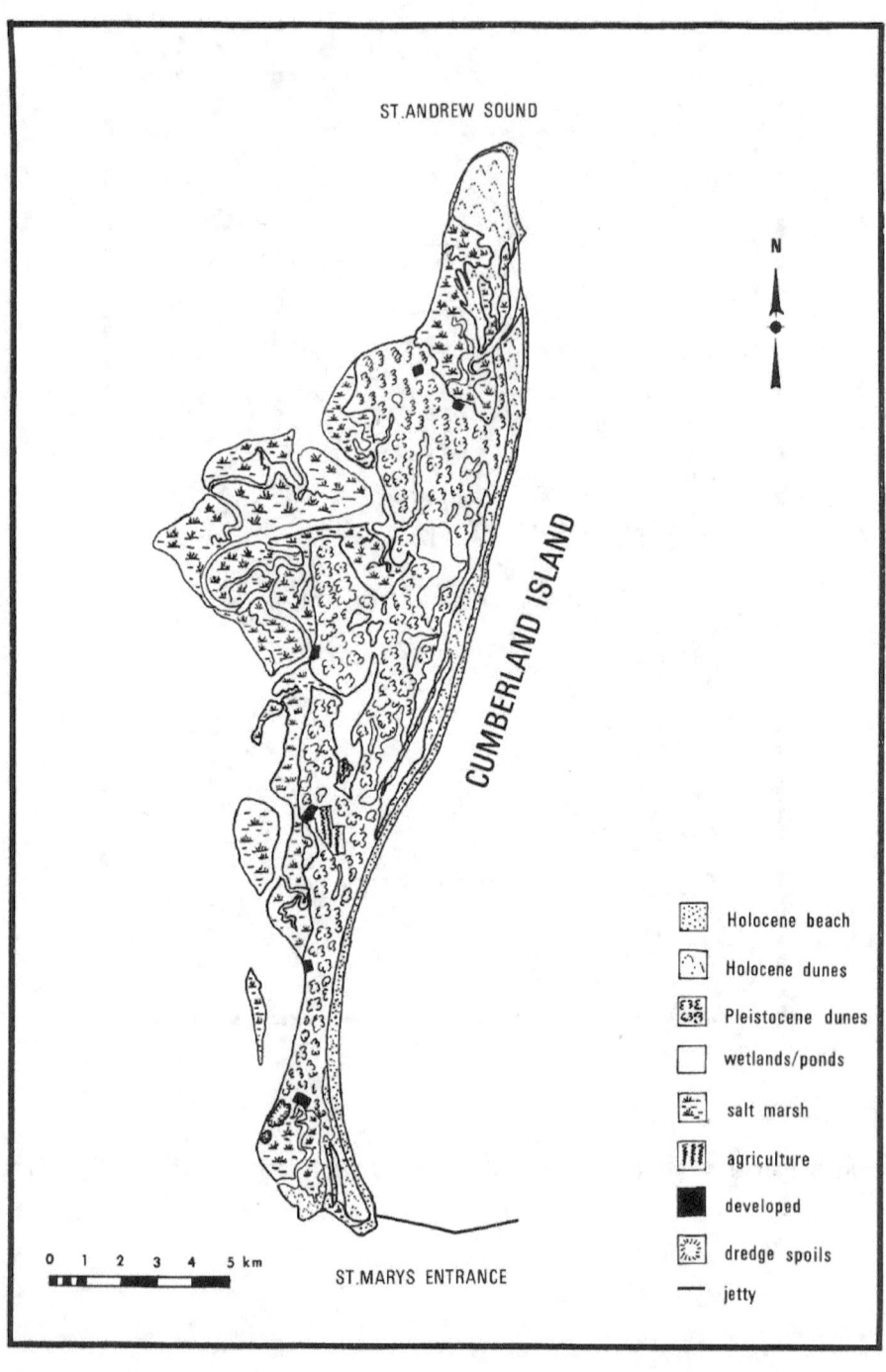

Figure 4. Map of the geomorphology (landforms) of Cumberland Island.

he *stratigraphy,* or layering of sediments, of Cumberland Island (fig. 5) was determined by xamination of drilling cores recovered from 18 bore holes. The ages of the various sediment ypes were determined by dating the fossils buried during sedimentation.

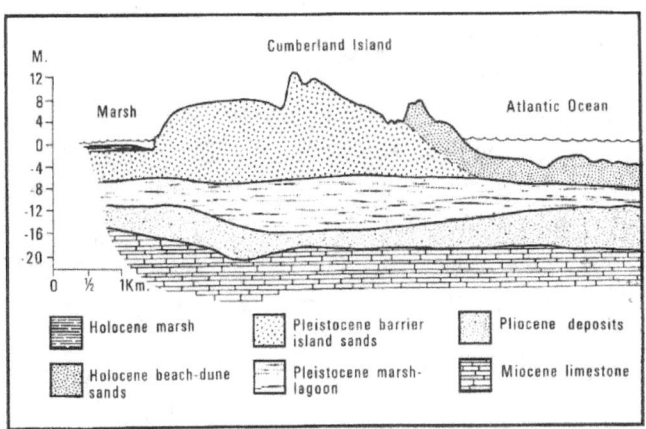

Figure 5. Diagram illustrating the stratigraphy, or sediment layers, of Cumberland Island.

he sea level fluctuations of the Pleistocene, followed by the slow rise of seas raised by ʒlacial meltwater, have shaped the sediments that form Cumberland into an island that rises ι7 m (56 ft) above sea level and extends 16 m (53 ft) under the sea to the ancient river ʤeposits upon which it rests. The Pleistocene "core" of the island consists of sands and clays. ʌ thin veneer of Holocene sands forms the present day beach dune environment and ∂xtends seaward as a sheet sand.

Rising seas both removed and reworked the beach sands, causing the island to build up ∨ertically as it moved closer to the mainland. Consequently, the Pleistocene marsh ;ediments that once formed the back-barrier environment are now buried 10-18 m (33-59 ˙t) below the old Pleistocene dunes of the interior and the younger (Holocene) beach dune ;ystem. Under the ancient marsh clays lies a thin 6-10 m (20-33 ft) layer of river sediments. ˙hese river sands were deposited about 15 million years ago (Pliocene Epoch) when the ;horeline was some 48 km (30 mi) inland. This entire sequence of sediments, in turn, rests jpon a much older Miocene limestone deposit, which formed in an open ocean environment ∨hen sea level was higher and the shoreline much farther inland.

GEOLOGIC TRAIL GUIDE

The geologic trail, composed of eleven stops, is designed to acquaint the curious visitor wit
tangible evidences of both the geologic history and the present day geological setting c
Cumberland Island. Because the walk is confined to a very small segment of the island
photographs taken on other National Park Service trails are included in the guidebook t
increase your familiarity with Cumberland Island. The entire walk covers close to 16 km (1
mi) and should only be undertaken as an all day endeavor to allow adequate time fc
enjoyment. If the two longer segments of the trail (Jetty Stop #6 and Dredge Spoils Stop #1C
are omitted, the walk is shortened to about 5 km (3 mi) and should serve as a pleasant an
educational morning or afternoon activity. The general location of stops is shown in figure €
please note that most of these trails are unmarked and refer to the National Park Servic
map to Cumberland Island (available at the Visitors' Station) for existing marked trails.

STOP 1: The Maritime Forest

The mature *maritime forest* seen between the Visitors' Station and Sea Camp is flourishing ir
the sands of the old Pleistocene beach ridges. It is dominated by centuries old, gnarled an
twisted live oaks, their limbs adorned with resurrection fern. The resurrection fern gets its
name from the way it can lose more than 70% of its water, look dead, and "resurrect" wher
it rains. The undergrowth here consists almost entirely of saw palmetto. There is little plan
diversity here in this "climax forest", the end result of the natural plant succession
condensed below:

Life Cycle of Typical Field	Years
Abandonment after farming.	0
Weedy annuals come in.	1
Perennials dominate (Broomstraw).	2
Pines dominate, palmettos below.	50-100
Deciduous trees, mainly oaks.	150+

In younger fields and forests of Cumberland Island (figs. 7-8), there is a large variety of trees,
including laurel oak, American holly, southern magnolia, red bay, southern cedar, water oak
and slash pine. Forests of picturesque, Spanish moss draped live oaks and slash pines are
now growing on the lands once cultivated for cotton and indigo. The very large slash pines
seen on Cumberland Island are rare on most of Georgia's other sea islands due to the
selective logging of the last few decades.

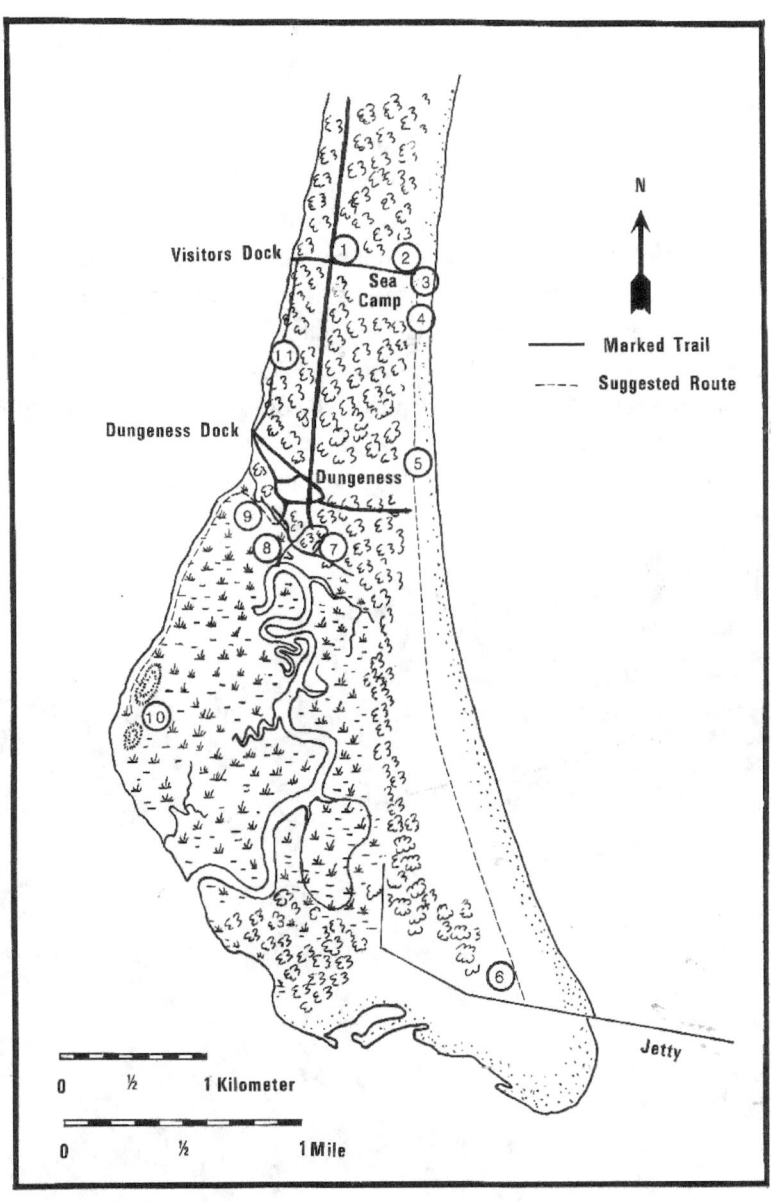

Figure 6. Guide to the Cumberland Island Geologic Trail.

STOP 2: The Boardwalk at Sea Camp.

As you mount the boardwalk from Sea Camp, you cross the sharp interface that separate the mature maritime forest of the interior from the actively changing beach dur environment stretching before you to the waters of the Atlantic. Before advancing, stop an look back into Sea Camp, and you will see a wind blown sand deposit that is slowly spreadir inland into the forest. Why is this sand here? When human, animal (non-native horses, cow pigs, etc.) or vehicular traffic destroys the anchoring vegetation of the sand dunes, the dur fields can be breached by a *blowout* which results as the steady, sand laden wind deposi sand landward and enlarges the opening. The ultimate result is beach erosion. Th boardwalk has been constructed to minimize the blowout and prevent others from formin The beautiful sand dunes of Cumberland Island would not exist in their present form if traff to the beach was not severely restricted. How do these dunes compare to those seen o other islands where buildings exist at the dune line and traffic through the dune fields unrestricted?

Figure 7. Abandoned rice paddies at Duck House Trail.

ick up a handful of dune sand and you will see a fine, well sorted (small variation in grain ize) sediment primarily composed of quartz sand grains. The dark, extremely fine grains are he "heavy minerals" so called because they are considerably heavier than quartz grains of he same size. Their origin lies in the Georgia Piedmont, from which they have been ransported by rivers to the coastal zone. These heavy minerals (rutile, epidote, hornblende, arnet) are frequently sorted and concentrated by wind and wave activity into distinctive atterns. Large deposits of these "heavies" are mined commercially in the Coastal Plain erraces as important economic minerals.

Figure 8. Maritime forest on Pleistocene dune ridge at Willow Pond Trail.
Note dune shape preserved at left.

STOP 3: Dune Fields

3A: Back Dunes

You can readily see from the boardwalk that there are three distinctive dune environments between the maritime forest and the beach (fig. 9); these include the *back dunes,* the *foredunes,* and the low lying area between them known as the *interdune area.* Dunes are formed when wave action brings sand above sea level, where wind activity reworks the sand into dunes. Coastal dunes develop where there is a sufficient supply of sand, and where a dominant, strong onshore wind is present. Building to the very tops of the live oaks of Sea Camp, the back dunes create a mighty barrier to storm wave erosion. The destruction of anchoring back dune vegetation by domestic horses, cows, and swine has caused these huge dunes to be pushed westward by the prevailing winds into the maritime forest in many areas of the island (fig. 10). These striking dunes are the most prominent landforms on Cumberland Island.

Figure 9. Beach dune environment including (left to right) foredunes, interdune meadow, and back dune ridge at Sea Camp Beach.

Figure 10. Back dune ridge migrating inland through the maritime forest at central Cumberland Island.

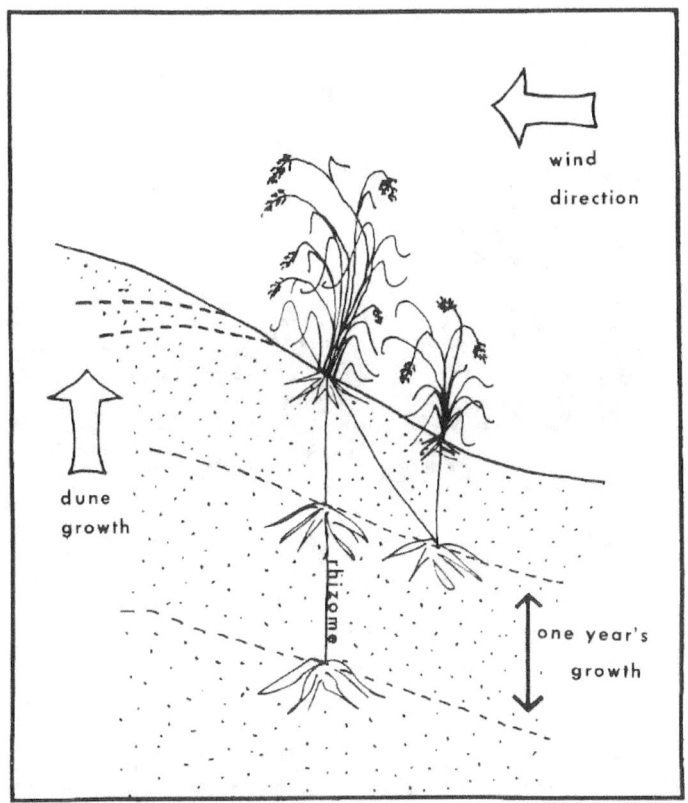

Figure 11. Role of sea oats in stabilization of dune sands. Note that the deeply buried rhizomes form an effective anchoring system for sand dunes.

Sea oats (Uniola paniculata), which both trap and anchor the sand, are vital to back dune construction. The deeply buried *rhizomes,* or root masses, form such an essential anchoring system (fig. 11) that they are protected by Georgia law.

3B: Interdune Area

This low lying area was formed as wind picked up the lighter sand of the foredunes and transported it to the back dunes, resulting in a shallow depression (fig. 12) between the two dune systems. When this zone is well vegetated, as on the southern end of Cumberland Island, it is called an "interdune meadow." Note that the wax myrtles appear to be leaning backward toward the back dunes. This phenomena, a result of plant growth retarded by salt spray, is known as *salt pruning.* Close inspection of the mighty live oaks will reveal that they, too, have been shaped by salt spray. The panic grass, salt meadow grass, and other vegetation of the interdune meadow form an important grazing area for island wildlife.

Figure 12. Wax myrtles of the well vegetated interdune meadow of Sea Camp Beach leaning landward due to the effects of salt pruning.

3C: Foredunes

This foredune field, considerably smaller and less stable than the back dune field, forms the first line of defense to storm wave erosion. In addition to the sea oats, "pioneer" plants such as panic grass, sea croton, and marsh elder here trap windblown sand. Notice how small immature dunes are forming behind little clumps of vegetation or shell accumulations (fig 13). These *wind shadow dunes,* which form through accumulation of sand behind a wind baffle, are the most common dunes of the Atlantic coast.

The burrows scattered through the foredunes are those of the ghost crab; these crabs decrease in size seaward, as may be seen in the decreasing burrow diameter.

Figure 13. Immature wind shadow dunes forming behind wind baffles created by the sea croton and horseshoe crab shell, foredune area of Sea Camp Beach.

TOP 4: Beach Zone

The broad, gently dipping area between the seaward edge of the foredunes and the offshore bar is known as the *beach zone*. Because the beach slope is controlled by sand grain size (the larger the grain size, the steeper the slope), the wave action has built a very gentle slope from the fine sands of Cumberland Island. A typical beach profile (fig. 14) consists of the previously described dune ridge, the *berm,* the *beach face,* and the *low tide terrace.* The appearance of the beach at this reading of the guide will depend on (1) whether the beach is presently depositional (fair weather profile), erosional (storm profile), or intermediate (ridge and runnel system) and (2) the stage of the tide.

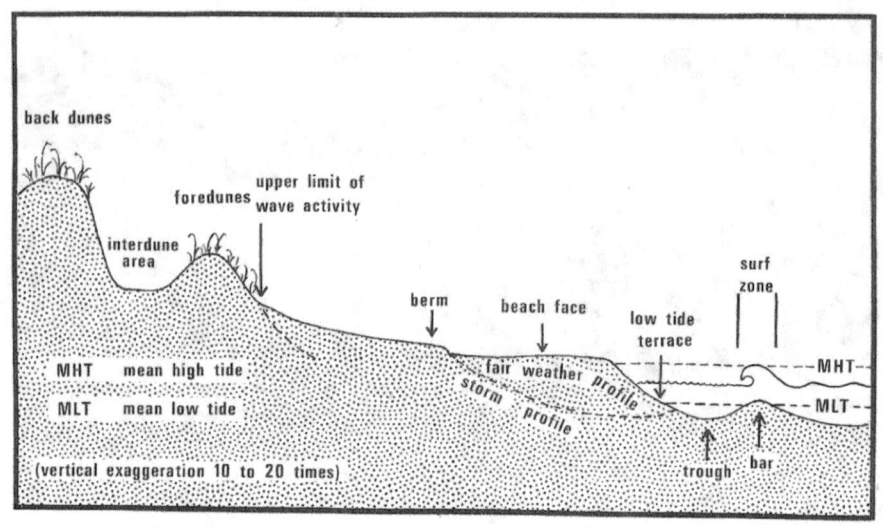

Figure 14. Beach configuration changes as a function of wave conditions.

As seen in figure 14, a beach under storm wave attack loses a large amount of sand; it i
recognized by a simple, concave upward beach face. As the storm removed sand i
eventually returned from offshore storage by wave action, *a ridge and runnel syster*
develops (fig. 15). The ridge is a large, landlord migrating crest of sand, and the runnel is th
shallow depression landward of the ridge.

The immediate width of the beach will depend upon the stage of the tide. The Georgia coas
has a tidal cycle of two high tides and two low tides a day, produced as the earth rotate
under the bulges of water shaped by the gravitational pull of the sun and moon. Extrem
spring tides (highest "highs" and lowest "lows") result at new and full moon. The smalles
neap tides (lowest "high" and highest "lows") occur at first and second quarter phase of th
moon. The extent of storm induced erosion is directly related to lunar cycle. A storm surg
occurring at a "spring high" in this environment of moderate to high tidal range can do a
much damage as a hurricane at a coast of small tidal range.

Figure 15. Large ridge and runnel system migrating inland on the beach at central Cumberland Island. Note the layering of heavy minerals on the ridge and the ripples in the runnel.

The beach also may be referred to as "a river of sand" because of the net downdrift (southwest) movement of sand produced by *longshore drift* and the *longshore current.* Because the dominant wind from the northeast causes the waves to strike the shore at an angle, a net downcoast transport of sand is produced (fig. 16). The same phenomenon of the waves' striking the coast at an angle results in a longshore current in the zone of breaking waves, or *surf zone* (fig. 16). You yourself have likely had the experience of entering the surf zone to swim or "ride the waves" only to find yourself downdrift of your beach towel in a short while.

The two most common beach structures are ripples and layering of the beach sediments. The layering is caused by concentration of the heavy minerals or by differences in grain size. Ripples, formed by both waves and currents, are present in the nearshore area. Their size varies widely, but their crests are usually parallel to the beach slope. When structures such as these are preserved in ancient sandstones, they provide a valuable key to aid in the study of geologic history.

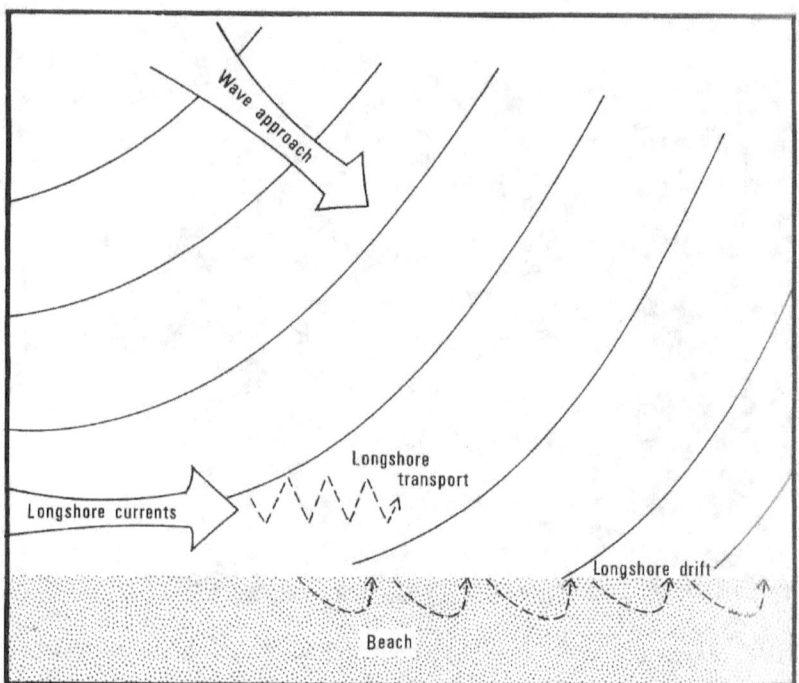

Figure 16. Longshore sediment transport. When a wave moves toward the beach at an angle, sand is lifted by the surf and moved diagonally up the beach slope. The backwash then carries the sand back down the beach at right angles to the shoreline, transporting the sand along the coast in a zigzag pattern. Sand is also moved underwater in the breaker zone by this action.

STOP 5: Sea Camp Beach to Dungeness Beach
Walk toward the edge of the water and pick up some damp sand. How does it compare to the dune sand? You can see that this sand is considerably coarser, darker, more poorly sorted (larger variation in grain size), and richer in broken and eroded shell material, or *shell hash*. Remember that the dunes are formed of wind blown sand and, therefore, only the smaller grains are selectively transported to the dunes.

Look landward and you will be able to discern the *high tide swash line,* the most landward of the wave-reworked sands. The swash line on this island is generally well marked by a reed-like deposit, the detritus of the salt marsh cordgrass. Close inspection reveals a pattern of tiny, curved sand ridges which reveal the farthest encroachment of the waves. Coarser but lighter material, such as broken shells, seaweed, or salt marsh detritus, accumulate along these ridges.

Now look seaward and determine the direction of wave approach and estimate the wave height. In these latitudes, the wind is predominantly from the northeast and the northwest the winter, from the south in spring and summer, and from the northeast in the fall. These prevailing winds coincide with the direction of the surface currents. Because the northerly winds of the winter and fall are much stronger than those of summer and spring, net longshore transport of sand is to the southwest. Wave height depends on the wind velocity, the length of time in which the wind is active, and the fetch, or distance, over which the wind blows. Average wave height at Cumberland Island is 23-31 cm (9" to 1 ft). There is little net movement of water in surface wave activity; rather, there is a propagation, or transfer of energy, between the water molecules. The movement of the water as a wave passes is circular in deep water and elliptical in shallow water. When waves approaching shore "feel bottom", they both slow and steepen. When the wave height exceeds one half the wave length, the waves topple over and break; these breaking waves form the surf zone (fig. 17). The *geomorphology,* or physical structure, of Cumberland Island is largely determined by the combined energy of wave activity and tidal currents.

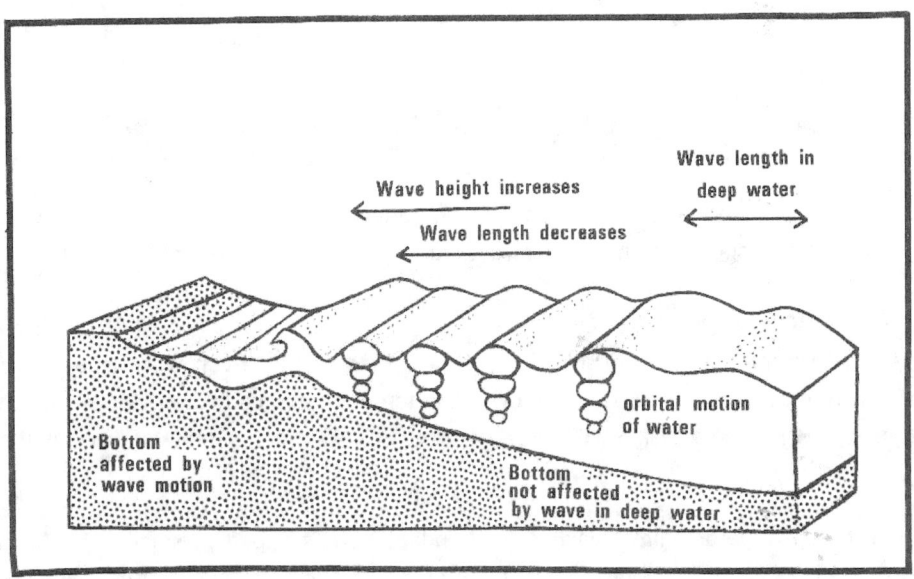

Figure 17. Nearshore wave configuration changes. As a wave approaches shore, several changes result as the orbital motion of the water interacts with the seafloor. The wave length decreases due to frictional drag, and the wave height increases as the water stacks up on the shallow seafloor. The water ceases to move in an orbit, breaks and rushes up the beach face.

STOP 6: Jetty

Construction on this jetty (and the corresponding one across the inlet on Amelia Island) was initiated in 1881 and completed in 1904 to aid navigation in the St. Marys River inlet (fig. 18). The jetty has served as a barrier to the southward downdrift transport of sand, causing the addition of approximately 2 km² (494 acres) to the south end of Cumberland Island (fig. 19).

Another consequence is that Amelia Island, deprived of sand that would have bee[n] transported there under natural conditions, has suffered considerably more erosion tha[n] Cumberland Island. Because jetty construction invariably causes updrift deposition an[d] downdrift erosion of sand, the practice has been largely discontinued in recent years b[y] coastal engineers.

Figure 18. Jetty located on the south end of Cumberland Island. Because the jetty acts as [a] sediment trap, the island has enlarged considerably updrift of this location.

STOP 7: Dungeness Wells: Water Supply

Many park visitors express curiosity about Cumberland Island's fresh water supply. The[y] wonder where the feral horses drink and why the tempting pumped water is labelled "unfi[t] for drinking" while the artesian well water, reeking of sulfur fumes, may be drunk withou[t] purification.

Fresh surface water for animal wildlife is abundant here, trapped m small ponds in the depressions between the old Pleistocene dune ridges. In addition, Lake Whitney represents a shallow .34 km² (84 acre) lake system unique to Georgia's barrier island system.

For human use, well water is pumped from two types of *aquifers*. An aquifer is a geologic unit which both contains and transmits water. Aquifers must be both porous (high percent of pore space) and permeable (readily transmit fluids); they are most often sands, sandstones, and limestones. An aquifer must be confined by layers of impervious material, such as clay or shale, to hold the water (fig. 20). Note that the *water table* is the zone below which groundwater has saturated the aquifer, filling 100% of the pore space with water. The *recharge zone* is the area at which the aquifer is exposed at the surface; here rainwater refills and "recharges" the aquifer.

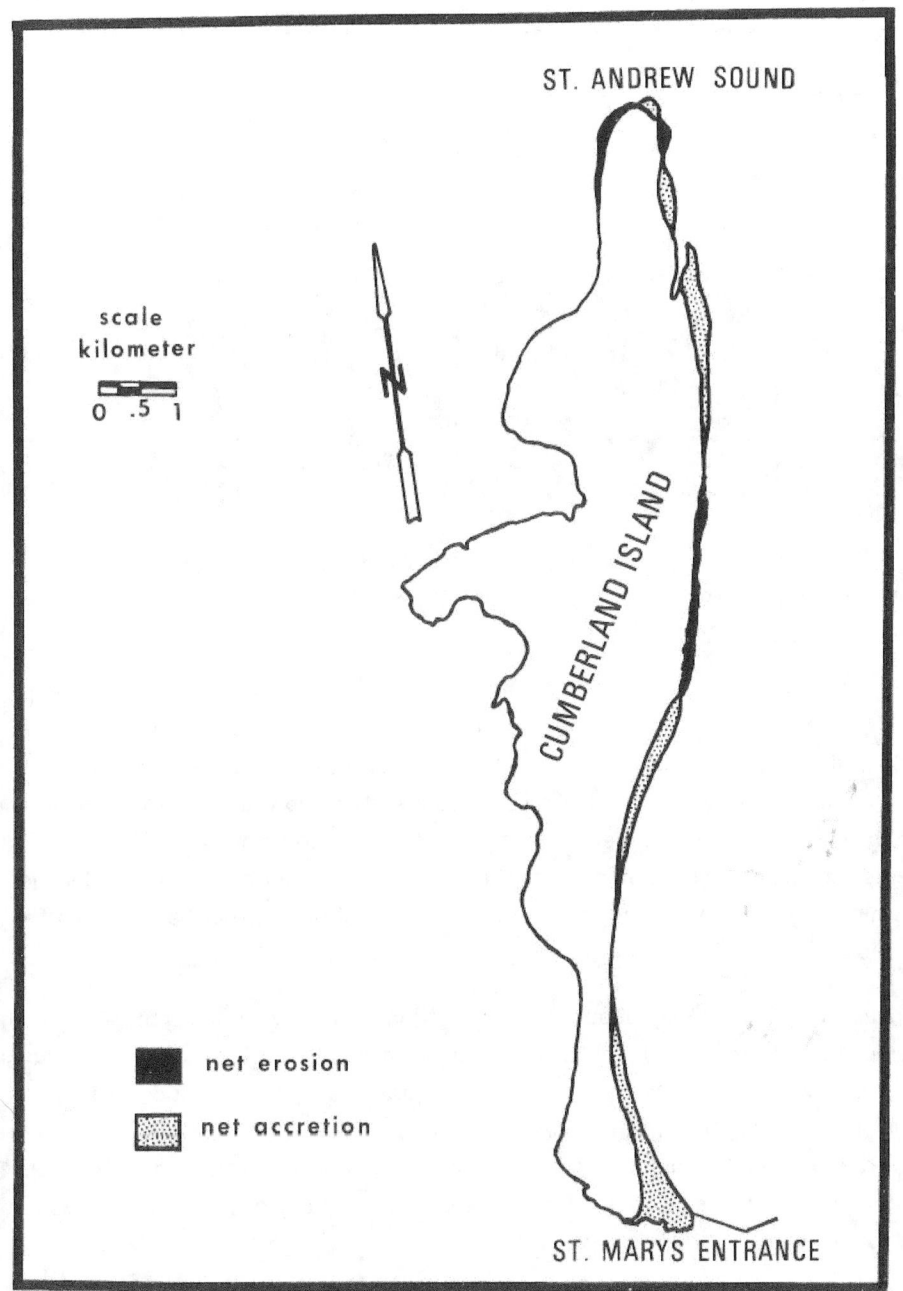

Figure 19. Shoreline changes on Cumberland Island, Ga., 1843 to 1974. Note updrift instability due to inlet migration and downdrift accumulation of sand due to jetty interrupted longshore transport.

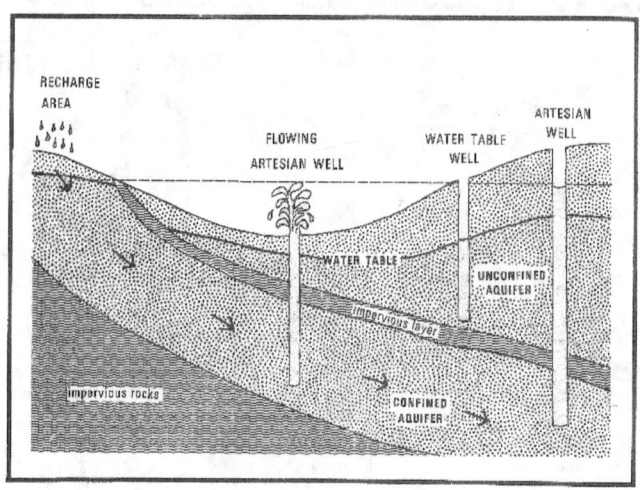

Figure 20. Geologic conditions which form confined and unconfined aquifers. Arrows indicate direction of groundwater flow in the confined aquifer.

Notice in figure 20 that wells may exist at several depths in the same area, and this is th case on Cumberland Island. The shallower wells merely pump water up from the saturate sand above the now buried impermeable clays of the Pleistocene marsh. This source of fres water is known as an *unconfined aquifer* because the upper surface is open and subject t contamination. The water supply at Sea Camp is from this aquifer but has been purified fo human use.

The deepest wells penetrate about 150 m (500 ft) into the ancient limestone aquifer which underlies Cumberland Island. This extensive unit, known as the Principal Artesian Aquifer has an overlying impervious layer of clay which protects it from pollution; it is therefor known as a *confined aquifer*. It takes many hundreds of years for water to travel her underground from the broad recharge zone in the upper Coastal Plain (fig. 21). The limestone of this aquifer is mined for concrete where it crops out near Albany, Ga., at a elevation of 64 m (210 ft) above sea level.

Flowing artesian wells from the Principal Artesian Aquifer, symbolizing the presence an mystery of subsurface water, occur on Cumberland Island because the water is under stron pressure from the weight of the overlying water. This pressure is sufficient to force wate above the surface in a well drilled through the impervious layer into the limestone aquife (fig. 22).

The strong sulfur odor associated with the artesian well water on Cumberland Island is due to hydrogen sulfide gas, formed by the decomposition of organic matter or by the reduction of sulfate minerals in water. This gas comes out of solution when the water surfaces, releasing a strong sulfur odor. The water is nevertheless well suited for drinking purposes; it is even naturally fluorinated within the limits set by the State of Georgia.

STOP 8: Indian Middens

These accumulations of oyster shells, numerous on Cumberland Island, represent the leavings of countless oyster feasts of the Timucuan Indians, who inhabited this island for more than 3,000 years. *Middens,* common features in the Georgia coastal zone, may be in the form of either large mounds or "shell rings." Shell rings also exist in the marshes of Cumberland but are now inaccessible by foot.

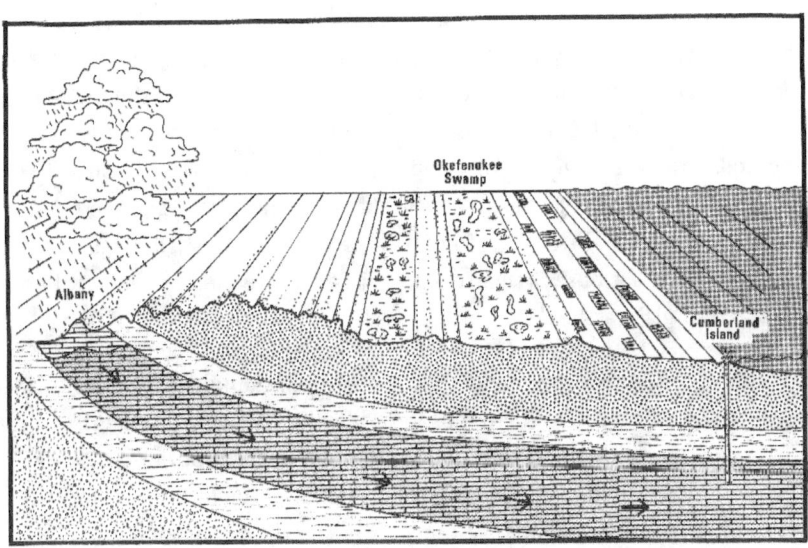

Figure 21. Diagrammatic representation of the geologic conditions resulting in artesian flow on Cumberland Island. Arrows indicate direction of flow for the groundwater.

Figure 22. Capped artesian well on Yankee Trail, flowing freely.

Because the limestone of the oyster shells produces a high pH (alkaline) soil unfavorable to most island vegetation, the middens endure for long periods of time, unobscured by vegetation. When middens begin to weather into the soil horizon and thus "sweeten" the acidic island soil, they are vegetated by cedar trees, which flourish in alkalai soils. Most cedars on Cumberland Island will be seen in the marsh fringing forests, the environment in which Indian middens are invariably found. Sites of ancient shell rings are frequently recognized by the very curious, circular clumps of cedars frequently seen on barrier island remnants in the Georgia marshes.

Cumberland Island residents have made good use of their abundant legacy of oyster shells. The extensive *tabby* construction (fig. 23), seen today in the older dwellings and walls, was produced by a simple, but highly practical and durable, mixture of burned oyster shells (to make lime), sand and water. In addition, the middens were mined for use in road construction and for the dike and dam systems necessary for rice production.

Figure 23. Tabby construction seen at the old ice house at Dungeness. The extensive use of tabby by early Cumberland Island settlers made good use of the abundant oyster shell middens.

STOP 9: Salt Marsh

As you leave the shade of the maritime forest, you quickly overstep another sharp interface and enter the salt marsh environment. Look seaward and you will se the large back dunes which are encroaching upon and encompassing oaks and palms. The extensive maritime forest of Sea Camp does not exist here, suggesting that this narrow zone of the island was once a channel for the St. Marys River. Looking landward you will see extensive salt marshes directly before you and across Cumberland Sound (fig. 24). Salt marshes are normally found in protected intertidal waters behind barrier islands or within estuaries (where fresh water meets ocean water). Marsh sediments are fine grained silts and clays, and vegetation is restricted to salt tolerant plants.

Figure 24. Salt marsh zonation seen from River Trail. Note high marsh in foreground and low marsh in background. The white area is an old oyster reef.

Zonation of vegetation is determined by elevation, which controls the depth and duration of flooding by saline waters (fig. 25). The high marsh environment, located on the marsh edge closest to the island, is dominated by the black needlerush (Juncus roemerianus). Other common plants include spike grass, sea ox eye, salt meadow grass and glasswort. The low marsh, viewed across the sound, is dominated by the long cordgrass (Spartina alterniflora), which produces two crops per year. The marshes and estuaries of Georgia represent one of the most naturally fertile areas in the world; the net production amounts to about 10 tons (dry weight) of organic matter per acre per year.

Both marsh zones are densely inhabited by swarms of fiddler crabs, whose burrows and pellets blanket the surface of the marsh. Periwinkle snails and mussels thrive in the low marsh, feeding at low and high tide, respectively. Deer and feral horses graze in the high marsh (fig. 26), while raccoons feed in both.

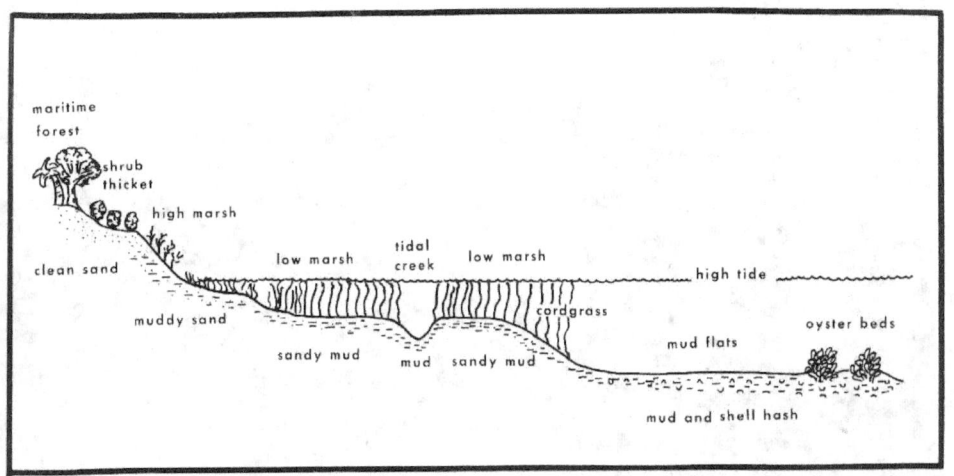

Figure 25. Typical marsh and tidal flat system illustrating zonation of surface sediments and vegetation. Mud flats and oyster reefs are exposed at low tide.

The oyster community marks the edge of the marsh complex. It influences the deposition of the fine grained sediments, for feeding oysters secrete a mucus that binds the sediments together. Additionally, the oyster reef contributes a large amount of shell hash to the system.

Salt marshes, long considered worthless, are now known to he highly productive ecological systems. Better than 80% of all edible sea life is spawned or hatched in this "nursery of the sea." Additionally, organic matter from the marshes, washed out by the tides, feeds ocean fish.

Before leaving this marsh area, note the old oyster reef exposed before you. Compare this location to the one shown in figure 25. What does this suggest about relative changes in sea level and/or the landward migration of Cumberland Island?

Figure 26. Feral horses grazing on the salt meadow grass of the high marsh. Wild turkeys and deer feed here as well.

STOP 10: Dredge Spoils: Fossil Collecting

Note: This 3.2 km (2 mi) round trip walk through the marsh is recommended only for foss collectors willing to travel at a good pace during low tide. (Check tide tables posted at Se Camp). Tennis shoes or boots must be worn for protection against prickly pear spines an oyster shells buried in the marsh. Only experienced hikers should attempt fossil collecting a these sites; because Grand Avenue has been surfaced with spoils material, the keen eye collector may spot many shark teeth on walks along the main road.

The spoils material was dredged out of Cumberland Sound by the U.S. Army Corps o Engineers to facilitate boat travel in the Intracoastal Waterway. Spoils may be recognized a artificial mounds of sand mixed with large amounts of shell material and age blackene fossils. The best collecting sites are found in the more recent spoils.

Many vertebrate fossils have been found here, including shark teeth, ray plates, and turtl plates (fig. 27). Because the material has been thoroughly mixed in dumping, accurate datin is difficult, but most fossils are of Pliocene age, or from 1.8 to 5 million years old.

Figure 27. Shark teeth and sea drum teeth collected in the dredge spoils.

STOP 11: Back Barrier Environment

The forest just inland of the salt marsh, known as the *maritime strand forest,* is characterized by a soil rich in calcium, derived from Indian middens and old oyster reefs, and is subject to a high water table with high tide. In addition to the live oak trees, this forest is distinguished by cabbage palms and red cedars. The cedars, which can only grow in island soils whose natural acidity has been lowered by marine shells, have been harvested for pencils and other uses on many southern barrier islands.

As you walk toward the boat dock, notice that several large cedar trees, undercut by the bank erosion, have fallen onto the marsh sediments below, exposing old Indian shell heaps. How do these shells compare in density, position and weathering to those of the old oyster reef exposed in the high marsh?

If Cumberland Island is indeed retreating landward, what could account for the back barrier erosion seen here? Why should the oldest remaining dunes and their deeply rooted and anchoring trees slump over onto the marsh? Close inspection of the marsh surface will reveal many broken and weathered tree trunks, revealing the former position of the maritime strand forest. This back barrier erosion is the result of undercutting by tidal currents in Cumberland Sound, accentuated by the action of waves set in motion by boat traffic in the intracoastal waterway. This boat wake-induced erosion, extensive in coastal areas, is frequently unrecognized as a primary impact of man.

CONCLUSION

Cumberland Island offers its visitors a rare and precious gift, that of experiencing the wild beauty of a nearly undisturbed barrier island. Because it has been so little altered by man, the island represents an invaluable study area for geologists, biologists, and archeologists. It is obvious that the rich heritage of Cumberland Island deserves to be protected, as well as savored. Increased knowledge of the geologic history of this island, as well as the processes that shape it today, should increase your pleasure during this visit and your commitment to the conservation of its priceless heritage.

ACKNOWLEDGEMENTS

This guide was prepared for the United States Department of Interior as part of Contract No. CX5000-8-1563. Charles T. Swann, formerly of the Department of Natural Resources, initiated work on this guide. Thanks are extended to Marlene Finley of the National Park Service, Jim Sadd, Resident Marine Geologist of Fernbank Science Center, and Mildred W. Graham, President, Georgia Association of Marine Educators, for advice and critical review of this guide.

BIBLIOGRAPHY

Hayes, Miles and Kana, T.W., 1976, Terrigenous clastic depositional environments: Tech. Rept. No. 11, Coastal Research Div., Dept. Geology, Univ. South Carolina, Columbia.

McLemore, W.H., Swann, C.T., Wigley, P.B., Turlington, M.C., Henry, V.J., Nash, G.J., Martinez, J., Carver, R.E., and Thurmond, J.T., 1981, Geology as applied to land-use management on Cumberland Island, U.S. Dept. Interior Contract #CX5000-8-1563: Georgia Geol. Survey, Atlanta.

Office of Planning and Resources, (Resource Planning Section), 1975, Value and vulnerability of coastal resources: Georgia Dept. Natural Resources, Atlanta.

Walker, R.G., ed., 1979, Facies models: Geological Assoc. Canada, Dept. Earth Sciences, Univ. Waterloo, Waterloo, Ontario N2L 3G1.

Wharton, C.H., 1978, Natural environments of Georgia: Georgia Dept. Natural Resources, Atlanta.

GLOSSARY

Aquifer - A geologic unit that contains and transmits water.

Back barrier - The landward boundary of a barrier island characterized by salt marshes, tidal creeks, and tidal flats.

Back Dunes - The ridge of large dunes most landward of the beach, under natural conditions well vegetated and stable.

Barrier Island - An elongate island of sand or gravel built parallel to shore, forming a protective barrier between the mainland and the open seas, and separated from the mainland by a water filled depression.

Beach Face - The inclined surface of the beach which dips from the crest toward the water to a change of slope.

Beach Zone - A deposit of wave washed sediments along the coast between the landward limit of wave action and the outermost breakers.

Berm - A nearly horizontal portion of the beach formed by storm waves.

Blowout - A break in the dune line excavated by the wind when dune vegetation is destroyed.

Confined Aquifer - An aquifer bounded by impervious layers and therefore protected from pollution.

Collision Coast - A coast formed where two plates converge.

Ebb tidal Delta - Underwater accumulation of sand built by the falling tide.

Estuary - A bay at the mouth of a river where fresh water mixes with, and dilutes, the sea water.

Flowing Artesian Well - A well in which the confined ground water is under sufficient pressure to rise above the top of the aquifer in a well.

Foredunes - The small ridge of unstable dunes just landward of the beach.

eomorphology - General configuration of the earth's surface.

igh Marsh - The salt marsh, dominated by black needlerush, that lies
oove high tide but is occasionally wetted by a storm swollen tide.

igh Tide Swash Line - The most landward of the wave-reworked sands.

iterdune Area - The shallow depression between the back dunes and the foredunes; when
ell vegetated, known as the interdune meadow.

ongshore Current - A current in the surf zone moving parallel to the shore.

ongshore Drift - A zigzag, parallel to shore movement of sand which results when waves
ush sand up the beach at an angle and the backwash moves it straight down the beach
ice.

ow Marsh - The salt marsh, dominated by the long cordgrass, which lies between the high
nd low tide marks.

ow Tide Terrace - A terrace, below the berm, built by wave washed sediments.

Maritime Forest - The evergreen oak dominated climax forest of the coastal island uplands.

Maritime Strand Forest - The back barrier maritime forest of oaks, palms, and red   cedars;
he soils are enriched by calcium from marine shells.

Middens - Heaps or rings of oyster shells accumulated through numerous Indian oyster
oasts

Neap Tides - Tide of decreased range which occurs about every two weeks when the moon is
t 1st quarter or 3rd quarter (minimal gravitational effect).

late Tectonics - The theory of global dynamics in which the lithosphere is believed to be
roken into individual plates that move in response to convection in the upper Mantle.

Recharge Zone - The area at which an aquifer is exposed at the surface; here water is added
o the groundwater reservoir.

Rhizome A subterranean mass of roots that produces shoots above and roots below.

Ridge and Runnel - A large, landward migrating crest of sand with a narrow depression
andward of the crest.

Salt pruning - Plant growth shaped by the effects of salt spray.

Shell Hash - Broken and eroded sea shells.

Spring Tide - Tide of increased range which occurs about every two weeks when the moon is full or new (maximum gravitational effect).

Still stand - Relatively constant sea level.

Stratigraphy - The composition and sequence of geologic units.

Surf zone - The zone of breaking waves.

Tabby - A cement of burned oyster shells, sand, and water used extensively by early barrier island settlers.

Tidal Range - The difference in height between successive high and low tides.

Trailing Edge Coast - Where the opposite continental coast is a collision coast (Amercia trailing).

Unconfined Aquifer - An aquifer in which the unconfined ground water will not rise above the water table in a well; water in such aquifers is subject to contamination.

Water Table - The upper surface of the groundwater saturated soil or rock.

Wind Shadow Dune - A sand dune that forms through the accumulation of sand behind a wind baffle.

Publications Editor/Coordinator: Eleanore Morrow